The Kindness Kids

Maryln Appelbaum and Stephanie Catlett

Illustrated by: Stephanie Catlett

Thank You From Maryln:
Thank you so much to all of you that work with children and make a difference. Thank you Stephanie for your hard work and for your great idea and illustrations that brought Kindness Kids to life. Thank you to our wonderful Appelbaum team led by Marty Appelbaum who work so hard to make this world a better place for children. Special thanks to our ATi team member, Renè Bloom, for the many hours she spent editing the book.

Thank You From Stephanie:
Thank you to the Appelbaum Training Institute, educators, and parents, for the many hours you invest to enrich the lives of children. You are amazing! Thank you Marty Appelbaum and Maryln Appelbaum for the honor of sharing this project with you. Your incredible support and gentle guidance means so much. It is so much fun working with the ATi team. Thank you all! It is a privilege to work with you, Swedo. Thank you for your devotion to this project. You are so talented. Thank you for sharing your time. To my husband, Scott Catlett, and to my Mom, Ruth, thank you for your encouragement, love and support. I could not do this without you. And to my children, Seth and Seleste, kindness is a choice. You can choose to be kind to everyone. Thank you for being kind. You inspire me.

Published by Appelbaum Training Institute, Inc.
104 Industrial Boulevard, Suite A
Sugar Land, TX 77478
Text copyright © 2013 by Maryln Appelbaum and Stephanie Catlett
Illustrations copyright © 2013 by Stephanie Catlett
Distributed in USA by Appelbaum Training Institute, Inc.
104 Industrial Boulevard, Suite A
Sugar Land, TX 77478
Printed in USA
All rights reserved
ISBN 978-0-9892990-1-5

Today is a very special day!
Today is Micah's first day of child care.
He's excited.

Miss Tracy is Micah's teacher.
She introduces Micah to the whole class.
Micah is happy to meet new friends.

Micah sees a little boy named Chucky looking sad and standing all by himself.

Micah asks Chucky if he is okay because he is not singing with the other children. Chucky says, "I feel lonely and I'm sad."

Micah tells Chucky that he will be his friend and play with him.
Chucky is so happy that he claps his hands
and has a big smile on his face.

During circle time, some of the kids get up to dance.
Micah sees a little girl named Megan sitting in a wheelchair.
She looks sad.

Micah goes over to her and says,
"Can I dance with you?" He pushes her little wheelchair back
and forth in time with the music. She is so happy that she giggles.
Micah looks for ways to help others and make them smile.

Miss Tracy says, "It is time to go to learning centers." Micah chooses to go to the art center. There is a class project to make noise makers. He sits next to Caleb. Caleb does not understand English very well and looks sad.
Micah says, "I will help you," and he shows Caleb what to do.
This makes Caleb so happy that he gets a big smile on his face. It is fun to help others.

Now it is time to go outside. The class lines up.
Little Timmy gets in line. He is smaller than the other kids.
One of the children walks over to him and pushes him.
Timmy cries.

Micah sees Timmy crying.
Micah lets Timmy get in line ahead of him.
Timmy smiles. Micah is so kind.

When the children come inside, it is time to
wash their hands and eat lunch.
Miguel is the first to sit at the lunch table, but he looks really sad.

Micah sees he is sad and sits next to him.
He asks Miguel why he is so sad. Miguel says, "Kids make fun of me.
Someone took my cookie away and said I was too fat."
Micah said, "I will share my cookie with you."
Miguel smiles and says, "Thank you." Micah likes to be kind and share.

It is naptime. Micah sees Alex crying.
He asks Alex why he is crying.
Alex says, "The kids make fun of me because I wear glasses."
Micah says, "I like your glasses. I will be your friend."
Micah makes Alex feel better. He is kind.

When the kids are waking up,
Micah hears Ling and Jada whispering.
Ling says, "I wish I had different eyes so other kids would like me."
Jada says, "I wish I had lighter skin so no one would be mean to me."

They say to each other, "Let's be friends."
Micah hears them and says, "I want to be your friend too."
Ling and Jada smile.

After nap time, it is time for free play. Micah has an idea.
He asks Miss Tracy if it is okay to start a special club called
the Kindness Kids Club.
In order to get in the club, kids have to be kind to each other.
Miss Tracy says, "Yes, that's a great idea."

Miss Tracy tells the class they are going to do a very special art project.
She has them cut leaves out of green paper.
She tells them they are Kindness Leaves.

The children help Miss Tracy place a big paper tree on the wall.
She tells them that is their class Kindness Tree.
She says they are starting a Kindness Club.
To get into the club you just have to be kind to others.
Micah is so proud that she used his idea.

The class loves the Kindness Tree.
They all want to belong to the Kindness Club.
Starting now, they will all be kind to others
and help other children feel better.

To celebrate, they have a Kindness Party.
Everyone marches around the room saying, "I'm a Kindness Kid.
I'm kind to others. I help others smile and feel better."

Miss Tracy says, "Let's learn the Kindness Cheer.
Do you want to learn the cheer?"

The class shouts, "YES!"

"Here is how the cheer goes!"

K-I-N-D

that's the way we want to be,

BE KIND oh yeah,

oh yeah, **BE KIND**

WOOOOOOOOOOOOOOOOOOOO!

The class starts cheering with Miss Tracy. It is fun!

After they learn the Kindness Cheer, everyone takes turns saying kind things to each other.
When they are finished, Miss Tracy writes each of their names on a leaf to place on the Kindness Tree.

The children each get a certificate that says they are in the
Kindness Club. It is great to be in the club.
You can be in the Kindness Club too!

Do you want to be a Kindness Kid like Micah and his friends?
It's easy to join the Kindness Club.
Say kind things to your friends. Teasing, hurting, and making fun of others is not kind, and will keep you from being in the club.
Kind words are the best words to share with others.

Kindness Kids are so special.
Join Micah and be a Kindness Kid today and
help others smile and be happy.

The Kindness Kid's Club
Official Member

Awarded with pride to:

_____

For being kind to everyone.

Date: _____

This certificate may be reproduced for non-commercial purposes only.